This edition published by Concordia Publishing House
3558 South Jefferson Avenue, St. Louis, MO 63118-3968
1-800-325-3040. www.cph.org
Scriptures taken from the HOLY BIBLE, NEW INTERNATIONAL VERSION
Copyright © 1973, 1978, 1984
International Bible Society
Used by permission of Zondervan Bible Publishers
(paraphrased for young children)

Getting Ready for
Christmas

A Daily Advent Prayer &
Activity Book for the Family

written by Yolanda Browne
illustrated by Patrick Girouard

CONCORDIA PUBLISHING HOUSE • SAINT LOUIS

Getting Ready for Jesus to Come

The time leading up to Jesus' birthday is called the season of Advent. Advent is from a Latin word that means "coming." This season focuses on the coming of the Savior. It begins on the Sunday closest to November 30th and ends on December 24th, the day we celebrate Christmas Eve.

We use the time during Advent to get everything ready to welcome Jesus. Just as families prepare a room when a new baby is expected, God helps us prepare our hearts. How? By thinking about how wonderful God is to give us this special gift of His Son.

The days of Advent also give moms, dads, sisters, and brothers a special reason to pray together each day as a family.

They can share their excitement, look forward to receiving baby Jesus afresh into their hearts, and remember that Jesus will come again someday.

How to Use This Book

Every day, you and your family can read a page, pray together, then join in the family Advent activity.

In this way, you will keep God in all your Christmas preparations, count down the days until Jesus comes, and be ready to celebrate Jesus' birthday on Christmas Day.

Note to Parents
The Advent activities are for your family to enjoy together. Be sure to supervise little ones for safety's sake.

Gabriel Visits Mary

God sent the angel Gabriel to a town called Nazareth. There, he gave a message to Mary, a pure, unmarried young girl. "Greetings, Mary! God has chosen you! You are going to have a baby boy named Jesus. He is God's only Son!"

Luke 1:26–32

Today's Prayer

Thank You, God, for Your special plan for Mary. Thank You for Your special plan for me. In Jesus' name. Amen.

Advent Activity

Draw or cut out a picture of an angel for your Christmas tree.

My Shepherd

Micah said, "Out of you, little town
of Bethlehem, will come the greatest of rulers, for
He will be the Shepherd of all of God's people."

Matthew 2:6

Today's Prayer

*Dear Jesus, because You are the Good Shepherd, the
greatest shepherd of all, I know You take care of all my
needs. I am safe and sound. Amen.*

 Advent Activity

How does a shepherd look after his sheep?
Today make a sheep ornament.

Moon Beams

Praise Him, sun and moon!
Praise Him, all you shining stars!
God commanded, and there you are!

Psalm 148:3, 5

Today's Prayer

*Dear God, how You love light! There is no darkness in You at all.
Thank You for the sun that lights the day, the moon and stars that
light the night, and for Jesus, who lights up our hearts. Amen.*

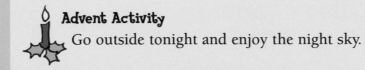

Advent Activity
Go outside tonight and enjoy the night sky.

Big Sky, Little Me

I am overwhelmed when I look up
at the heavens and see the stars Your
hands have made. It is amazing that
You even think about me!

Psalm 8:3–4

Today's Prayer

Dear God, Your world is so big and I am so small. Yet, You know me and give me everything I need. I may not always understand it, but I am grateful. In Jesus' name. Amen.

Advent Activity
Today make a star ornament.

No Room

Joseph and Mary needed to go to Bethlehem to be counted even though Mary's baby would soon be born. When they arrived, an innkeeper sent them to a stable because there was no room in the inn.

Luke 2:1–7

Today's Prayer

Dear Jesus, I think if the innkeeper had known God's Son was about to be born, he would have made room. Help me to always see You as You really are, God's Son, my Savior. Amen.

Advent Activity

Can you think of a time when somebody turned out to be different than you expected?

Bird Lover

Jesus said, "Look at the birds—they don't
buy or make their food and they don't
store it anywhere. God is the one who takes care of them.
You are even more valuable to God than the birds."

Luke 12:24

Today's Prayer

*Dear God, if birds are important enough for You to take care of,
I know You will take extra-special care of me. For Jesus' sake. Amen.*

Advent Activity
Set out a special Christmas feast for
the birds. Everyone loves a treat!

Heavenly Rest

God grants His loved ones sleep.

Psalm 127:2

Today's Prayer

Dear God, You are so wonderful—You give us everything we need, even sleep. Thank You for sending Jesus to me and for watching out for all Your creatures. Amen.

Advent Activity

The Bible tells us God never sleeps. Tonight, when you go to bed, thank Him for protecting you while you sleep.

Good Gifts

"If a child asks his parents for a fish, will
they give him a snake? Of course not!
If people, who are not perfect, know how to give
good gifts to their children, won't God, who is perfect,
do a much better job of giving good gifts
to His children when they ask Him?"

Matthew 7:10–11

Today's Prayer
*Dear God, You continue to give us good things. Thank You for being
such a kind and generous Father. In the name of Jesus. Amen.*

Advent Activity
Can you think of anyone who needs your
generosity this Christmas season? What can
you and your family do to help?

Jesus Loves Children

Jesus loves little children
and says His kingdom belongs to
them and those who believe like them.

Matthew 19:14

Today's Prayer

Dear God, thank You that we are all Your children—even grown-ups. Help us all to come to You and to lean on You like little children lean on their parents. For Jesus' sake. Amen.

Advent Activity

Look at your baby pictures. Do your mom and dad have pictures of themselves when they were little?

Make Way!

"Make way, you in the desert! Raise all
the valleys; level all the mountains;
smooth out the rough and rugged places.
Make a highway—the Lord is coming!"

Isaiah 40:3–5

Today's Prayer

*Dear God, make my heart ready for You. Forgive my sins for
Jesus' sake so that nothing will stand in Your way. Amen.*

 Advent Activity

As you prepare for Christmas, can you think of
anything in your life that might be rough or rugged
that you need God to smooth out?

Good Fruit

Years before Jesus was born, Isaiah, a prophet,
gave us a picture: Jesus would be like a new branch
growing out of an old stump. He would bear special fruit:
wisdom, understanding, knowledge, power, delight in God,
goodness, and justice. Amazing things would come
from Jesus because God's Spirit was with Him.

Isaiah 11:1–5

Today's Prayer

*Dear God, I know that I can never be perfect like Jesus, but please
help me to be like a tree that bears good fruit. For Jesus' sake. Amen.*

Advent Activity

Make an ornament shaped like your favorite fruit.
How can others "taste" the good fruit we bear?

The Shepherds' Surprise

There were shepherds living out
in the fields, keeping watch
over their sheep at night.

Luke 2:8

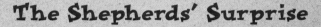

Today's Prayer

*Dear God, the shepherds were just doing their everyday jobs.
They could not know You had the most wonderful surprise
waiting for them. We look forward to all the surprises You have
waiting for us because of Jesus. Amen.*

Advent Activity

Make a list of all the good things God has already given you.

God's Lamp

God's Word is like a lamp that lights
the path of our lives by showing us
how to live in God's Truth.

Psalm 119:105

Today's Prayer

*Dear God, thank You for the Bible. Help us to grow in our love
and understanding of Your Holy Word. In Jesus' name. Amen.*

 Advent Activity
Shine a flashlight in front of you as
you walk. See how it lights your way.

Stand Up and Shine

Stand up. Shine and be happy, for the light
of Jesus has come into the world!

Isaiah 60:1; John 8:12

Today's Prayer

*Dear God, thank You for Jesus who lights up the sad
and dark places of our lives. Amen.*

 Advent Activity

Together light a Christmas candle in a darkened
room. See the difference? Use your candle at dinner
to remind you of the light of Jesus.

Living Well

Jesus said that everyone who drinks water
will be thirsty again. But the water that comes
from knowing Him will bubble and rush up
from inside us and form a well
that can never run dry.

John 4:13–14

Today's Prayer

*Dear God, help me to be content in Your love. Thank You for Your love
that fills my heart to overflowing. For Jesus' sake. Amen.*

Advent Activity

Place a glass underneath the faucet and turn the
water on full force. Watch it overflow. Can you
think of a time when your heart was overflowing?

Real Bread

Jesus said that He is our real bread.
We can never be hungry in our deepest,
inside places when we believe and trust in Him.

John 6:35

Today's Prayer

Dear God, thank You for filling me up with the love of Jesus so even when my stomach is hungry, the rest of me doesn't have to be. Amen.

Advent Activity

Make or buy some Christmas bread and give it to someone whose tummy might need filling.

Wise Men, Wise Gifts

God put a special star in the sky.
Some Wise Men who studied the stars
knew what this meant:
A new king had been born.

Today's Prayer

Dear Jesus, the Wise Men figured out You were the king people had been waiting for. They brought You king's gifts: gold, frankincense, and myrrh. Help me to be wise and believe in You, too. Amen.

They traveled a long way,
following the star of Bethlehem.
"We saw His star in the east and have come
to worship Him," they said.

Matthew 2:1–2

Advent Activity

What gift can you give Jesus?

Smarty Pots

Can a pot say to the one who made it,
"I know more than you do"?

Isaiah 29:16

Today's Prayer

Dear God, sometimes we think we know everything. We are sorry. Help us remember that You are in charge. Thank You. Amen.

Advent Activity

Make a pot-shaped Christmas ornament. Who is smarter—you or the pot?

Better Than Gold!

I love Your commands because
they are pure and right. They are more
precious than gold.

Psalm 19:9–10

Today's Prayer

*Dear God, thank You for making it possible for every single
person to be rich in blessings. Help us to follow Your commands.
For Jesus' sake. Amen.*

Advent Activity

Why is it better to be rich in who we are than
to be rich in what we have?

Real Treasures

Since our hearts are set on the things
we love, store up heavenly treasures,
which can never be stolen or harmed in any way.

Matthew 6:19–20

Today's Prayer

*Dear God, help me remember that the best treasure of all
is Jesus. He can't be lost or outgrown. He will be with me
forever. Amen.*

Advent Activity

Show your family your special treasures.
Can you think of some heavenly ones?

The World's Best Gift

Let us thank God for His priceless gift.

2 Corinthians 9:15

Today's Prayer

Dear God, help us to know You better. Thank You for sending Jesus. No one but Your own Son could have shown us what You are really like. Amen.

Advent Activity

There is not enough money in the world to replace a priceless gift. What makes Jesus our priceless gift from God?

Heaven's Door

Jesus said, "Here I am! I'm standing at
the door and knocking. If anyone can
hear My voice, open up and let Me in. We can
sit down and eat and be together forever."

Revelation 3:20

Today's Prayer

*Dear Jesus, You came from heaven to this earth to knock
on the door of my heart. Thank You for opening the door
to heaven for me. Amen.*

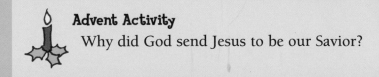

Advent Activity

Why did God send Jesus to be our Savior?

Announcing: Jesus!

Suddenly, the sky was filled with angels!
They were praising God and saying, "Glory to God
in the highest, and peace to everyone, for today
God has shown you how much He loves you!"

Luke 2:13–14

Today's Prayer

*Dear God, what a proud Father You are—announcing Your
Son's birth by filling the sky with angels. How wonderful of
You to send Jesus to make me Your precious child. Amen.*

Advent Activity

Today ask your parents to tell you the story
of what they did to announce your birth.

Jesus is Born!

Mary gave birth to her baby and laid Him in the manger. It was just as Isaiah had said: "A Child is born to us, a royal Son is given! He will carry all the authority of heaven and earth upon His shoulders. He will be called Wonderful Counselor, Mighty God, Everlasting Father, and Prince of Peace."

Luke 2:6–7; Isaiah 9:6

Today's Prayer

Dear God, You sent Your Son. We needed Him, and You sent Jesus to save us. Thank You so, so much! Amen.

Advent Activity

Take a little time to think about this first present of the Christmas season.

Oh, Come, All Ye Faithful

Oh, come, all ye faithful,
joyful and triumphant!
Oh, come ye, oh, come ye to Bethlehem.
Come and behold Him,
born the King of angels:
Oh, come, let us adore Him,
Oh, come, let us adore Him,
Oh, come, let us adore Him,
Christ the Lord!
Amen.

("Adeste Fideles" from J. F. Wade's
Cantus Diversi, 1751)